FBI ANECDOTES

MICHAEL M. BIASELLO

outskirts
press

FBI ANECDOTES
All Rights Reserved.
Copyright © 2024 Michael M. Biasello
v5.0

The opinions expressed in this manuscript are solely the opinions of the author and do not represent the opinions or thoughts of the publisher. The author has represented and warranted full ownership and/or legal right to publish all the materials in this book.

This book may not be reproduced, transmitted, or stored in whole or in part by any means, including graphic, electronic, or mechanical without the express written consent of the publisher except in the case of brief quotations embodied in critical articles and reviews.

Outskirts Press, Inc.
http://www.outskirtspress.com

ISBN: 978-1-9772-7650-6

Cover Photo © 2024 Michael M. Biasello. All rights reserved - used with permission.

Outskirts Press and the "OP" logo are trademarks belonging to Outskirts Press, Inc.

PRINTED IN THE UNITED STATES OF AMERICA

Table of Contents

First Arrest	1
First Interview	2
Humility	3
Cocaine	5
Riot	7
Random Street Scenes	10
Shooting	12
Distrust	20
Kidnapping	22
Bank Robbery	25
Hostages	28
Brothers	31
Police	33
Stripper	34
Justice	36
Innocence	38
Gang	41
Cowards	42
9/11	44
Abuse	46
Grief	47

I was born and raised in South Philadelphia, attended Saint Richard and Holy Spirit elementary schools, Bishop Neumann High School, and graduated from Villanova University in 1975, BA, Criminal Justice.

I entered on duty with the FBI on June 18, 1984, New Agents Class 84-14, and retired on December 31, 2010.

In my career, I was assigned to FBI Field Offices in Mobile, Alabama; New York City; Jackson, Mississippi; and San Antonio, Texas, Austin Resident Agency. I also served temporary duty assignments in FBIHQ SIOC; Greenville, North Carolina; Charleston, South Carolina; Dallas, Texas; Oakdale, Louisiana; and Seattle, Washington.

I was awarded the New York City Police Department Medal of Valor, the FBI Medal for Meritorious Achievement, as well as numerous commendations and recognition from the United States Attorney General and FBI Director for service and performance, to include, 9/11 investigative team, investigative work at Fort Hood subsequent to the terrorist attack, and the protection detail for United States Attorney General John Ashcroft.

Subsequent to September 11, I was one of ten agents selected by the FBI Director to investigate the hijackers, specifically, American Airlines Flight 77.

I have supervised a Fugitive Task Force, Organized Crime Drug Enforcement Task Force, and the National Center for Missing and Exploited Children Program in Jackson, Mississippi. I possess extensive investigative experience in terrorism, money laundering, homicide, kidnapping, bank robbery, fugitives, narcotics, Foreign Counterintelligence, and a myriad of federal violations.

I received the following training and Certifications: CIA Counterintelligence, FBI Foreign Counterintelligence, Terrorism, United States Department of Justice Street Survival, FBI Emergency Vehicle Operators Course, Reid School of Interrogation, FBI Active Shooter Training, FBI SWAT Team Leader.

Subsequent to the FBI, I served as the first Director of Security at Ashley Hall School, located in Charleston, South Carolina.

I served as the Senior Investigator in the United States Attorney's Office, Pensacola, Florida. I was involved in the initial criminal investigation of the terrorist attack at the Pensacola Naval Air Station in December 2019.

Disclaimer incorporated pursuant to the FBI Prepublication Review Policy:

"In accordance with my obligations as a former FBI employee pursuant to my FBI employment agreement, this book has undergone a prepublication review for the purpose of identifying prohibited disclosures, but has not been reviewed for editorial content or accuracy. The FBI does not endorse or validate any information that I described in this book. The opinions expressed in this book are mine and not those of the FBI or any other government agency."

I wish to express sincere gratitude to Lawrence A. Keefe, former United States Attorney, Northern District of Florida, and the Family of FBI Special Agent Leonard W. Hatton for their consent in this writing. All other names of individuals depicted and several locations have been changed to protect and respect privacy.

The following investigative anecdotes are in chronological order.

FIRST ARREST

FBI Mobile Division, October 1984
Mobile, Alabama

I reported to my first office of assignment, Mobile, Alabama and was assigned a Training Agent (TA). Within the first few days, the drug squad formulated the planning and tactical arrest of two narcotics dealers. As the arrest team assembled and prepared for the entry, arrest, and search of the residence, the TA and I were to observe from a short distance. The six man entry team was composed of three SWAT team members and three seasoned FBI agents. Prior to entry, one of the agents with whom I would become best friends, communicated on the radio, "get the new guy up here". As I took up the lead position, which was highly unusual and a deviation from standard FBI practice, I asked why and he responded, "you're the new guy, not married, no kids, expendable, and since you just got here from Quantico, you probably shoot better than most of us." The arrest occurred without incident.

This would be a portent of my career.

FIRST INTERVIEW

FBI Mobile Division
Fairhope, Alabama

In November 1984, I was assigned to a bank fraud investigation which required an interview of a female bank employee, Cindy Grande.

I approached Grande at the bank, identified myself, and asked to conduct the interview in a private office or conference room. Grande discreetly stated that she would prefer to be interviewed outside the office so as to avoid calling attention to her involvement. I agreed to an interview the following day at her residence. I arrived at her apartment in Fairhope, Alabama, Grande opened the door dressed only in a robe, untied at the waist, her left breast exposed. Grande invited me into her apartment. I told her we will do the interview later. Cross the threshold of the door, any and all allegations are on the table, FBI career terminated.

I wanted to return the favor. The following day I returned to the bank, approached the bank manager, loudly identified myself as an FBI agent presenting my credentials, and informed him that Grande was a witness in a federal investigation. Needless to say the interview was conducted without a problem.

I was certain I was going to enjoy this career.

HUMILITY

FBI Mobile
at Hayneville, Alabama

I was born and raised in South Philadelphia. Played pickup schoolyard basketball throughout Philadelphia, walked through the projects, been involved in fights going to and from high school, and lived in a neighborhood with organized crime figures. However, this city kid wearing a blue suit, white shirt and tie, was witness to an unforgettable experience in rural Alabama.

As a new agent in the Mobile Division, I was assigned to conduct interviews in a voter fraud investigation in Hayneville, Lowndes County, Alabama, population, a few hundred. Specifically, I was tasked to interview the residents to determine their ability to read, write, and sign their birth name. No one in the office wanted this assignment. I, as the new agent, was elected.

The people I was to interview were destitute elderly black people, living in poverty, modest homes composed of four cinder block walls resting on literally dirt floors, with chickens and a few farm animals roaming about in the Alabama heat. Initially, the residents were hesitant to speak as they considered me the "tax man". Once convinced I was an FBI agent, everyone was extremely welcoming.

I spent approximately one month, two two-week assignments, in Hayneville, Alabama, and interviewed well over 100 people. Engaged in many conversations, none of which concerned voter fraud. Invited and shared a mid afternoon lunch of red beans and rice at a couple's home. All were interested in my life and travels that landed me in Hayneviile as I was in their lives. Enjoyed every person I met.

All of these good people have since passed, but their friendliness, hospitality, and above all, honesty and humility, will never be forgotten.

A once in a lifetime experience.

COCAINE

FBI Mobile
Loxley, Alabama 1986

Organized Crime Drug Enforcement Task Force (OCDETF) investigation concerning Cubans transporting multiple kilos of cocaine interstate. This group was living and based in a farmhouse surrounded by several acres of farmland in Loxley, Alabama. Investigation necessitated photographs of all visitors, vehicles, and occupants entering and exiting the property. My partner, Howard, and I were to surveil the property for a week. Loxley, Alabama was extremely rural, acres and acres of kudzu and poison ivy.

Howard and I, in camo clothing, weapons, and photo equipment, established surveillance of the subject property in 105 degree heat, in the middle of an Alabama summer. The main road and the only road onto the property was blocked by an industrial steel gate which opened and closed manually. Surveillance began at 9 AM until late afternoon.

We belly crawled 150 yards through three foot high weeds up to the barbed wire fence line to obtain optimal photos. Progress was slow so as not to disturb the grasses and be visible from the house.

We heard a door close and voices. Binoculars enabled us to identify the two individuals as the primary subjects of the investigation. They began walking in our direction through the grasses. As they approached we remained stationary. We, specifically I, had inadvertently stopped on top of a fire ant mound. Within seconds, the fire ants had crawled through the forearm sleeve openings of my shirt. A hundred bites simultaneously. Forearms burning. Fortunately, the subjects stopped walking and continued their conversation within ten yards of our location. The subjects walked in the direction of the house, we were able to back track and exit the area. We successfully obtained photos of vehicles, individuals, and overheard details of their shipments which was integral to the probable cause for search warrants and eventual prosecution.

The subjects were transporting multi-kilo shipments of cocaine in the false floor of an 18 wheeler used as a cattle/pig transport in order to mask the scent of cocaine from K-9 detection.

Upon execution of a search warrant for the primary residence, twenty subjects were arrested. All were subsequently convicted in federal court and received lengthy federal prison sentences.

Forearms were swollen and ached for weeks.

RIOT

Federal Detention Center
Oakdale, Louisiana 1987

Catherine and I planned to be married on Thanksgiving Day, November 26, 1987. However, on November 21, 1987, a prison riot and hostage situation developed at the Federal Detention Center (FDC) at Oakdale, Louisiana. As a member of the FBI Mobile Division SWAT team, we were dispatched to FDC Oakdale with several other FBI SWAT teams and members of the FBI Hostage Rescue Team. The wedding was postponed.

In 1980, Cuban dictator Fidel Castro opened his prisons and shipped inmates to the United States, known as the Mariel boat lift. FDC Oakdale housed more than 1000 Mariel prisoners, mentally ill, criminally insane, and violent offenders, had taken 28 hostages, prison guards and inmates considered informants. The rioters were armed with prison made machetes, metal spears, and Molotov cocktails, during the eight day siege.

Walking the perimeter of FDC Oakdale, common to see inmates swinging machetes, taunting the agents, daring us to enter the prison. A few days in, the rioters threatened to set a hostage on fire, another inmate was attacked and chased by rioters armed with machetes. The inmate fled over the interior prison fence and jumped into the razor wire to avoid being hacked to death. Allegedly, he was an informant. Plans were underway to conduct a tactical entry as the lives of the hostages were increasingly in peril as daily negotiations failed.

*Aerial view of Federal Detention Center Oakdale,
Oakdale, Louisiana*

Thanksgiving Day was very cold. Dinner was served from a local food truck outside of the prison main gate. This was not a memorable meal.

On November 28, 1987, the inmates released the remaining hostages and surrendered. The Mobile SWAT team was tasked to clear and search several cell blocks for inmates hiding, weapons, contraband, and booby traps.

Inmate armed with machete
Oakdale, Louisiana

We entered the prison aboard an armored personnel carrier. The inmates had jammed the toilets causing the cell blocks to be flooded with two to three inches of human waste. To this day, I appreciate my SWAT issued Gore-Tex boots. The stench was overwhelming. The team wore surgical masks lined with mentholatum to tolerate the smell. Fortunately, the freezing temperature also helped to minimize this issue. The search of the cell blocks was slow and dangerous. Many of the bathroom stall doors had been locked from within and contained booby traps. One such trap was fashioned to fire a metal arrow as the stall door was breached.

A surreal experience.

Catherine and I rescheduled our wedding for December 3, 1987.

RANDOM STREET SCENES

FBI New York, circa 1990-1991

Surveillance in New York is unlike any other. Dangerous, sometimes entertaining. Tim and I set up surveillance at 40 th and Lexington Avenue. Found a prime parking spot at the intersection. Manhattan, specifically 40 th Street and Lexington Avenue, is a high volume area. Tens of thousands of pedestrians and as many vehicles, most of which are taxis. Businesses, restaurants, bars, sandwich shops, significant activity all of the time. On this day, at approximately 1:30 PM, as we waited for our subject to move, Tim and I observed an elderly bag lady, filthy, bags in each hand, dress dragging on the sidewalk. She stepped off the curb and entered the intersection on a diagonal. She hobbled to the center of the intersection causing traffic to cease, cabbies yelling curse words, the middle finger in the air, car horns blaring, pure traffic mayhem. The lady stopped, hiked up her dress, squatted in a sitting position, and urinated in the intersection in full view of Manhattan. Car horns blaring louder, some taxis edged forward threatening to run her over. Unbelievable scene. Only in New York. When finished, she dropped her dress, walked to the curb, and down the sidewalk, never to be seen again.

FBI New York
Circa 1990

Another surveillance, 1 st Avenue, approximately 75 yards south of 34 th Street. At 10:30 AM, facing northbound, a six foot tall perfectly proportioned, shapely woman, slowly strolls past my Bureau car wearing nothing but a straw sun hat and stiletto heels. Dave (the designated squad photographer) and I only saw her back but we were determined to get to the intersection so we could enjoy a full frontal. I floored the accelerator, disregarding speed limits and arrived at the intersection of 1 st Avenue and 34 th Street as Dave readied his camera. As luck would have it, a parking space was available for a good view.

However, this was not at all what we expected. Dave and I unfortunately witnessed a full grown mature male strolling naked, no doubt after a night of New York City debauchery.

FBI Jackson, Mississippi

A confidential informant was meeting a dealer for a "buy-bust" of a kilo of crack cocaine for $20,000. There had been two previous sales.

The deal was to happen in a hotel parking lot in Jackson off of I-10 at 7 PM. I agreed to meet the CI at the hotel at 6 PM.

We went to the hotel mens room to prep for the meeting. The CI stripped down to his underwear and stated, "Got some bad news today, doctor told me I was HIV positive." I stopped the preparation and asked, "Why didn't you tell me sooner?" He shrugged his shoulders.

We finished the preparation for the drug buy. The subject arrived in a pickup, the transaction occurred at the driver's window. When the CI cleared the parking lot, agents surrounded the pickup and arrested the subject. As the arrest and search was conducted, an elderly couple approached, the woman asked, "What's going on? Drugs? I nodded. She responded, "If you ask me, kill'em all".

SHOOTING

FBI New York
New York City, Midtown 1991

On Wednesday March 20, 1991, I and four FBI agents planned to conduct a physical surveillance in Midtown Manhattan from 7 AM to 3 PM. The participating agents are identified as follows: SA Jeffrey Phillips, SA William Regan, SA Joseph Edwards, and SA Julian Garza. At approximately 6 AM, as I approached the Holland Tunnel toll booth, I realized that I left home without cash and was unable to pay the $4.00 toll. I made a U-turn to find an ATM in Jersey City. However, as luck would have it and my fortune on this day would reveal, I drove through Jersey City and Hoboken unable to find an ATM that was operable. Desperate to get to the team meeting point, I identified myself as an FBI agent and showed him my credentials. He refused entry and insisted that I could not pass without paying the toll. I told him I was driving through, as I pulled away he handed me an envelope to submit payment either by mail or in person to the toll booth taker at my next opportunity.

At approximately 7 AM, I met with the agents to discuss the surveillance. Prior to establishing a specific assigned surveillance position, I borrowed $5.00 from Agent Phillips and bought a coffee. At that time that was the total amount of money in my possession. At approximately 8 AM the subject of the surveillance exited his residence and entered his vehicle. While the other team members surveilled the subject, I located an ATM at the Bowery Bank on East 42nd Street and Park Avenue and withdrew $20.00. I returned to the surveillance team location and established a visual surveillance of the subject. I advised the other surveillance units of my specific location, 30 th Street approximately 100 yards west of 1 st Avenue. Agent Regan and Agent Garza were parked northbound on 1 st Avenue near 30 th Street and Agent Edwards and Agent Phillips were parked northbound on 1 st Avenue at East 33 rd Street.

At approximately 11:30 AM, while seated in my vehicle and double parked outside of NYU Medical Center, near the intersection of 30 th Street and 1 st Avenue, I maintained the visual surveillance of the subject walking among hundreds of pedestrians. While maintaining a visual on the subject, I observed in my drivers side mirror, a Hispanic male (Mario Mezcal), approach from the rear of the vehicle. I noticed he was in his late 20's, approximately 6' and 150 pounds, thin build, narrow face, dark hair. I also observed that he was wearing a baggy canvas jacket, dark green in color, dark baseball cap, and dark shirt. He reached through the open driver's window with his left hand, grabbed me by the collar and with a gun in his right hand hit me in the left temple with the barrel of the gun inches from my left eye. The gun was a black semi-automatic pistol. Simultaneously, he said, "Motherfucker, give me your wallet or I am going to blow your fucking face off". Reacting, I grabbed the barrel of his gun with my right hand and grabbed his hand which was gripping the gun. We struggled for a few seconds, I realized that in order to disarm him I would have to bend his wrist and the gun across my face. I felt this was too dangerous and shoved his arm and the gun out of the window. He again banged the barrel against the side of my head, I said, "Okay, okay, here's my wallet." With my left hand, I unbuttoned my left rear pocket, removed my wallet and gave it to him. As I removed my wallet, I saw a second male (Joseph Ramirez) sitting in the driver's seat of another vehicle to my right. Ramirez was triple parked beside me and slightly forward to box me in. Ramirez had his driver's window down and although my passenger window was up, he was yelling to Mezcal, "Kill the motherfucker, kill the motherfucker." Mezcal pushed the gun within inches of my left eye, grabbed me by the collar, and constantly repeated, "Come on motherfucker, give me the cash." At this point, based on his increasingly violent actions and threats, I decided to look for the first opportunity to shoot him.

FBI car, newspaper used to conceal firearm.

I was trying to get my hand into my right front pocket for the $20 I withdrew from the ATM, but the Smith and Wesson .357 and holster were blocking my hand. Mezcal reached into the car with his left arm, the pistol against my left cheek, and grabbed my handheld radio off of the console. I was certain he would ID me as law enforcement. He shoved the radio into a pocket of his coat. He again reached across my chest to grab my right pocket. As I looked down, his left hand was scratching at my pocket, inches from my .357. I looked at Ramirez, seated in his car, hoping he could not see that I was armed. I told Mezcal that I'll get the money and he moved his left hand. I was able to grab the $20 bill and gave it to him. I then tried to remove change from my left front pocket but most fell onto the drivers side floorboard. Ramirez continued to yell, "Kill the motherfucker". Mezcal grabbed me by the collar, yanked me toward the window, put the gun to my left temple and said, "Motherfucker, I'm going to blow your fucking face off in five seconds". Mezcal began to count, one, two, as he looked over the top of my car to check for eyewitnesses, and as he said 'three', I drew my Smith and Wesson .357 and double-tapped him pointblank into the center of his chest.

I recall seeing Mezcal's shirt billow upon impact. Mezcal stepped back, our eyes met, I expected to be shot as a reaction to him being shot, his gun still pointed at my face, he began to run westbound on 30 th Street through traffic. I turned to shoot Ramirez through the passenger side window but he floored the accelerator and fled into traffic eastbound on 30 th Street. I exited my car and chased Mezcal approximately 75 yards westbound on 30 th Street at which time he dropped in the street.

I stood over him as he gasped for air. I picked up my Bureau radio and immediately called for backup. A Federal Express employee approached, I told him to stay away. He said, "Officer, I saw what happened. I was in my truck. You did the right thing. Can I help you?" I told him to tell the police what he saw. A second individual approached and offered assistance, I asked him to direct traffic. Incredibly, as I stood over the subject with my gun drawn, an elderly woman, apparently oblivious to the shooting, approached from between parked cars and asked me for directions. I told her to "get the fuck out of here." Meanwhile, NYPD had arrived and established a crime scene. I knew I did the right thing.

Deceased clothing.

Paramedics arrived on scene, cut the subjects clothing and attempted resuscitation. Mezcal was transported to Bellevue Hospital and pronounced dead. SA Garza accompanied the paramedics to Bellevue and recovered the $20 bill and my wallet. These items, which included a photograph of my parents, were saturated with Mezcal's blood. All items were retained by the FBI as evidence. Subsequently, the second subject was arrested at his residence and charged with Assault on a Federal Officer and firearms violations. This individual pled guilty and was sentenced to six years incarceration in the Federal Bureau of Prisons.

Five days after the shooting, I met with the FBI Shooting Review Team dispatched from FBIHQ for a mandatory interview. The interview was conducted in the FBI Newark Division, Red Bank Resident Agency Office. I related the events of that day, confident I took the correct action.

As required in any death investigation in Manhattan, a grand jury was convened. I was represented by Assistant United States Attorneys, Roger S. Sanborn and David W. Hamilton. At our initial meeting, they asked that I relate the facts of the incident. Still nervous from the incident, I told them the story of that day. As I finished, they also were clearly visibly upset.

View of 30th Street and scene.

FBI car.

MM's firearm, Browning Hi-Power 9 mm.

November 1992, FBI New York Office, FBI award ceremony, author Tom Clancy and FBI Director William S. Sessions.

The grand jury inquiry unnecessarily lasted until November 1991, as the Assistant District Attorney grasped in futility to create a case of an FBI agent's use of excessive deadly force. To no avail, in November 1991, the Manhattan Grand Jury issued a No Bill and the matter was forever closed.

Roger S. Sanborn and David W. Hamilton were excellent, professional, exceptional people. I was in good hands and forever thankful for their guidance, assistance, and friendship.

In November 1992, I was awarded the FBI Medal of Meritorious Achievement by FBI Director William S. Sessions, accompanied by author Tom Clancy. A week later, I attended a law enforcement award ceremony hosted by New Jersey Governor Christine Todd Whitman, and New York City Mayor Rudy Giuliani, and was awarded the New York City Police Department Medal of Valor in honor of New York City Police Officer Michael J. Buczek, killed in the line of duty in 1988.

DISTRUST

FBI New York, Fall 1991
Safehouse

September 1991, six months after my fatal shooting, I was selected to a security detail to protect "Joey", a New York organized crime hitman turned government witness. There were active and known contracts on his life.

The FBI secured a multi-acre estate as the venue for his protection. The property was pristine. Two story stone mansion, landscaped acres filled with trees and views of the countryside. Immaculate. To accommodate Joey, the FBI purchased and installed a new Nautilus home gym. Virtually on a daily basis, Joey hand wrote supermarket shopping lists for agents to purchase preferred imported Italian foods and delivery of his laundry, to include, silk pajamas to the local laudromat.

On any given day, Joey held court with agents listening to his war stories like school girls around the football jock. Their infatuation was sickening. Their fawning behavior, entrusting him, was dangerous and could potentially endanger everyone involved in this assignment.

I was raised in South Philadelphia. I grew up with and around street guys like Joey. I didn't like him, he knew it. The feeling was mutual.

During a weekend shift, on a Sunday morning, at 2:40 AM, I walked to the top of the second floor stairway, complete darkness except for the ambient TV light. I walked halfway down the stairs and saw the FBI agent "'on duty", sleeping in the fetal position on the sofa. The agent's service weapon was on the coffee table. Joey sat in a chair watching TV within arms length of the agent's weapon.

The agent's negligence, complacency, incompetence, and misplaced trust could have gotten us killed. An admitted hitman within inches of an FBI firearm. Inexcusable. I woke the agent and handed him his weapon.

Monday morning I walked into the FBI New York Office and informed the squad supervisor of the security incident. I withdrew from the assignment.

KIDNAPPING

FBI New York Office, 1992

Assigned to the FBI New York Joint Bank Robbery Task Force, my first investigative assignment was the kidnapping of an Israeli exchange student, Abraham Rosen.

On May 4, 1992, just after midnight, Abraham Rosen, an Israeli exchange student living in the Bronx, attempted to withdraw cash from an ATM machine near his residence. As Rosen left the bank, he observed an individual in the shadows. Rosen got into his car but was immediately subdued by two men, Anthony Provaci and James Moran. In the car, Rosen was blindfolded and pushed onto the passenger floorboard between Moran's legs. At one point, while driving to New Jersey, Moran attempted to blind and kill Rosen with a knife so he could not identify them. Moran was forced to stop the assault as the car approached the manned toll booth. Provaci and Moran forced Rosen to withdraw cash from several banks in the Bronx and New Jersey. Provaci and Moran, then returned to the Bronx with Rosen remaining pinned to the floorboard. Provaci and Moran brought Rosen to a basement apartment in the Bronx. In the apartment, Rosen was thrown on the floor, hands and legs duct taped together, kicked, and beaten in the face and head. Rosen was left lying on the bathroom floor. Throughout this ordeal, incredibly, Rosen remained lucid and retained details: Moran covered with green and gray tattoos; a detailed description of the apartment, red carpet, paneling, a kitchen floor with white linoleum and blue stars; a scalloped toilet seat; a telephone number; and a third accomplice, later identified as Bobby Lamana. After being held in the apartment for more than twenty hours, Rosen was discarded and found submerged in six feet of water in a Bronx sewer. The JBRTF responded, FBI Special Agent Leonard W. Hatton conducted the extensive and involved retrieval of forensic evidence and testified at the subsequent trial of Moran.

On July 9, 1992, Provaci pled guilty to Conspiracy to Kidnap and Kidnapping, and was sentenced to five years imprisonment contingent upon his cooperation and testimony. Since Provaci, Moran, and Lamana were low level mob associates, Provaci requested and was granted placement in a federal government security program. Provaci was incarcerated pending trial for Moran in the Metropolitan Correctional Center (MCC) in Lower Manhattan for debriefing.

All visitors, to include federal law enforcement, entering any federal prison and federal courthouse, are required to deposit their firearm in a lockbox. As Provaci was a cooperating government witness, he was housed with other Confidential Informants on one level segregated from the general population for security reasons. During one particular debriefing interview, I heard loud banging, yelling, toilets flushing, cursing, and death threats. The inmates on the upper levels stuff and flush the toilets so that the human waste runs down onto the CI segregated floor. MCC was placed in an immediate lock down. Provaci advised this happens at least once a week. Isolated and locked in a MCC cell, concrete and steel, with a violent felon, in proximity to other violent felons, unarmed, for an indefinite period. Thankfully, the MCC Correctional Officers who escorted Provaci to the cell for the interview, hustled me down the stairwell, through several corridors, to the MCC lobby and exit.

Moran was arrested on May 27, 1992 and advised of his Miranda Rights. A career criminal and street wise, he had nothing to say. Approximately three hours later, at the federal courthouse, Moran volunteered the statement, "You ain't got shit. All you got is a stinking snitch."

Moran had recently been released from Attica for a conviction for shooting two NYPD officers during a domestic violence call. Anticipating their arrival, Moran jumped out of a closet, shot the two officers, and was wounded himself in the firefight. Moran was released in February of 1992, three months prior to this kidnapping.

One day prior to this trial, while incarcerated at the MCC, Moran was involved in a cafeteria fight in which he slashed another inmate in the face with a pencil, cutting him open from below his ear to his chin.

The following day, trial commenced in United States District Court, Southern District of New York. Inasmuch as federal agents are prohibited from carrying firearms in federal courthouses, agents are required to store their weapons in a lockbox in the courthouse lobby. However, given Moran's history of violence and recent attack at MCC, I requested the Assistant United States Attorney to request authorization from the presiding trial judge that I be permitted to be armed in the courtroom. Permission was granted.

On the morning of Moran's trial, Bobby Lamana pled guilty and was sentenced to 22 years in federal prison. Minutes later, as the U.S. Marshals escorted Moran into the courtroom for his jury trial, he abruptly stopped at the prosecution table and said, "I'm going to kill you motherfucker".

On November 19, 1992, James Moran was convicted of Kidnapping and Conspiracy to Kidnap. Moran was sentenced to 30 years in federal prison. Moran was released in February 2020. Moran's current location is unknown.

BANK ROBBERY

New York, June 1992

FBI New York Joint Bank Robbery Task Force (JBRTF), received information from a Confidential Informant (CI) that a group of organized crime associates were planning a multi-million dollar bank robbery in Lower Manhattan. The CI was tasked to obtain more specific information: name/location of the bank, identities of all subjects, and, if possible, approximate time of day the robbery was to occur. Several days later, the CI provided the requested details, to include, the name/location of the bank.

In preparation for the surveillance, we obtained consent from a building tenant to place a lookout (LO) on a nearby office building overlooking the bank entrance. The bank was registered as a national landmark with a granite facade and lengthy granite steps leading to the front entrance.

The surveillance/arrest team was situated in a non-descript laundry van approximately 50 yards from the bank, at the north end of the street near the intersection.

CI advised that the subjects had cased the bank several times and were knowledgeable of a large cash delivery on Friday at approximately 1:30 PM. The surveillance/arrest team arrived at the designated location at 10:30 AM. In order to maintain our discreet position, the van engine was off as we waited in the van. Each team member was in communication with the LO via earpieces, and armed with a Bureau issued Sig Sauer 9 mm semi-automatic pistol, and either a 12 gauge shotgun or a Heckler and Koch MP 5 semi-automatic rifle. We were to maintain stationary positions, adhering to little to no movement and sound.

At 12:30 PM, the LO advised that the known subject was observed in the vicinity of the bank and walking on the sidewalk conducting counter surveillance. At this location in Lower Manhattan, pedestrian and vehicular traffic is constant, most of the time gridlock. The team was cognizant of the firearms and tactical issues when operating in this environment. The LO provided continuous updates to the team regarding the exact movement and location of the subject conducting counter surveillance.

The LO reported the subject was exercising extreme caution and was a professional. The LO advised that the subject had crossed the street and was in close proximity to our van location. Subject stood for inordinately long periods observing the street, people, and vehicles. Subject would take several steps, stop, and again observe all civilians and vehicles. LO advised the subject was fixated on our van and stood within arms reach. All arrest team members virtually suspended breathing as beads of sweat rolled off having stood in a van for three hours in June wearing ballistic vests and FBI raid jackets.

The LO advised the subject approached the van, placed his hand on the side of the cargo area and leaned on the van so as to detect any movement within. Imperative to maintain radio silence, lack of movement, and operational protocol so as not to compromise the operation. LO advised after a minute or so, the subject proceeded down the street and continued his counter surveillance. After approximately 45 minutes the subject walked to the corner diagonally across the street from the bank and placed a phone call and engaged in a conversation. The subject then proceeded to his vehicle and remained in his vehicle at the scene with a full view of the bank entrance. Several minutes passed, the LO advised that several known subjects identified by the CI as associates of the primary subject, were observed in various vehicles in the vicinity of the bank. The LO advised these individuals were observed in possession of long barrel/shoulder weapons and were wearing color coordinated navy blue windbreakers. Our tactical plan was to intercept the individuals on the entry steps to the bank so as to avoid a potential hostage situation in the bank involving bank personnel and civilians. The LO, given the height and location of the observation position, was able to clearly view oncoming traffic and vehicular movements.

At 1:30 PM, the LO advised the bank armored car was proceeding southbound approaching the bank. The armored car slowed as it passed our van and double parked in front of the bank.

The LO advised the subjects exited their vehicles with shoulder weapons partially concealed under their navy blue windbreaker jackets and walked among the hundred of pedestrians in the direction of the bank. The LO advised the two armored car guards exited the van and unloaded a large shipment of bundled vacuum sealed cash concealed in canvas bags onto a cart and proceeded toward the bank steps. As the guards lifted the cart up each step toward the bank entry, the subjects walked onto the lower portion. The team exited the van, FBI raid jackets and guns drawn, and ordered the subjects to the ground. Civilians entering and exiting the bank ran and dove onto the ground.

The armored car guards, initially oblivious to the approaching gunmen, froze in position. The adrenaline and intensity of the confrontation with armed subjects was tangible. The subjects, surrounded and outgunned, assessed the circumstances and potential consequences of a firefight, complied.

All subjects were arrested, entered guilty pleas, and sentenced to lengthy terms in federal prison.

HOSTAGES

FBI New York, 1993

While assigned to the FBI New York Office, we lived in a condominium in Plainsboro, New Jersey, approximately 60 miles from New York City. We could not afford a home closer to the city. The daily commute was at least two hours in the morning and two and half hours at night. Some nights I stopped on the New Jersey Turnpike for a nap and arrived home at 9 or 9:30 PM. Many agents lived further from the office: Easton, Pennsylvania; Upper Darby, Pennsylvania; Cherry Hill, New Jersey. Still others, spent their entire FBI careers in the NYO and endured that commute. Getting to the office was an adventure, particularly if you were not assigned a Bureau vehicle. In that case, the agent had to arrange and rely on other agents for the commute to the office and home. This always was problematic as agents were territorial of the Bureau vehicle and did not want to add an additional distance with another occupant to an already lengthy commute.

Fortunately, assigned to the New York JBRTF, agents were assigned a Bureau vehicle due to the nature of the work and in order to respond to an urgent call out.

At the end of a particular day, preparing to head home, the JBRTF received credible CI information that a group of Chinese, predominantly women, were taken hostage by a Chinese gang. The hostages were in the United States illegally, working menial jobs, and the gang saw an opportunity for extortion. The gang severed the ring finger or little finger of the hostages and delivered it or showed pictures to relatives of the hostage, demanding an extortion payment, usually between $15,000 and $30,000.

The search for the hostages continued well into the night. After midnight, the hostages were recovered in a basement in Queens. The JBRTF arrested seventeen subjects who were transported to the FBI NYO, 26 Federal Plaza, for fingerprinting and processing. During arrest and transport, the arrestees were hacking, coughing, and sneezing uncontrollably. The FBI nurse administered tuberculosis tests and confirmed each preliminarily tested positive for TB. Inasmuch as they had to be processed, each was masked for our safety. Given the large group to be processed, I was designated to take fingerprints. During the stages of processing, several of the arrestees, still handcuffed, intentionally removed the masks with their shoulder, nudging the mask below the mouth and continued hacking and coughing in our direction. Three, four, five in the morning, awake for over a day, dealing with TB carrying gangbangers intentionally disregarding commands, the agents involved were pissed off.

I had enough. These punks, who acted ignorant of English and defiant throughout the process, immediately grasped the English language and understood my "words of advice".

The processing was completed at approximately 6 AM, we headed home. At approximately 9 AM, I received a call to return as there was a hostage situation at a bank in Brooklyn. Awake for 30 hours already I knew this would not be resolved quickly.

The JBRTF arrived on scene and established a command post inside a nearby restaurant. NYPD blocked all streets and intersections in every direction. NYPD Emergency Services Unit (ESU) snipers were positioned atop the roofs diagonally across the intersection from the bank. FBI and NYPD negotiators attempted to establish telephonic communication with the subjects. Several hours passed with no progress when we received a call from inside the bank. One of the subjects wanted to surrender without the other's knowledge. He was instructed to exit the steel reinforced bank side door at exactly 1 PM and an agent would take him into custody. As the time approached, my supervisor and I left the command post to view the exterior of the bank and side door. NYPD ESU snipers armed with Ruger mini 14 rifles on bipods were in position, trained on the side door. A scene out of Dog Day Afternoon. The door was partially obscured by a tree and opened right to left which would prevent ESU from making an accurate shot. I approached the door, gun drawn, prepared. At 1 PM, the door slowly opened, the subject was ordered on to the cement facedown, handcuffed, and taken to the command post. During debriefing, he advised there were thirteen hostages, bank employees and customers. The hostages were held at gunpoint, not permitted to leave the lobby seating area or use the bank restroom, instead, they were given a large trash bag. His accomplice was armed with a sawed off shotgun.

An hour later, the hostages were released. NYPD immediately conducted a tactical entry of the bank and arrested the remaining subject without incident.

The defendants entered guilty pleas, each was sentenced to federal prison terms.

BROTHERS

New York JBRTF
Queens, New York, 1994

New York City in the early 1990's experienced an increase in violent and organized takeover bank robberies. These were conducted by professionals, armed with shotguns, and / or semiautomatic rifles, vaulting teller counters, getaway drivers, and adhered to a distinctive pattern and discipline. One such duo always wore black, established a pattern of robbing banks on Wednesday or Friday or both, between 1 PM and 3 PM. This duo was suspected of double digit bank robberies and brazenly hit the same banks repeatedly.

In the absence of any new lead information, the Case Agent (CA) and I as well as additional JBRTF vehicles conducted a surveillance on a known residence of a subject on a Wednesday afternoon. A short time later, the subject and another individual left the residence and drove a short distance to an apartment. They entered and returned to the vehicle with briefcases. We surveilled them for a half hour through a Queens neighborhood, pedestrians and street vendors everywhere. The subjects passed a particular bank three times which the CA mentioned had been robbed two previous times. As we surveilled them, the subject in the passenger seat flipped the visor down to use the mirror. He reached to the back seat and put a wig on, reached again and lifted a ballistic vest over his head, reached again and raised an Uzi machine pistol. Another violent bank robbery was imminent. The CA decided that we coordinate with the other JBRTF vehicles and ram their vehicle simultaneously in the front and back at the next intersection. We bumper locked their vehicle, when the traffic light turned green we rammed the rear of their car. They accelerated and turned the corner, foot traffic prevented us to follow. I jumped out and began running on the sidewalk parallel to the subjects. The subject vehicle also could not advance due to the pedestrians and the chaos of the cars colliding. The subject in the passenger seat saw me, raised the Uzi in a vertical position and smiled. I knelt down on the sidewalk and aimed. At that point, I heard a loud crash of metal, both subjects slammed against the dashboard. An agent jumped on the hood with an Heckler and Koch MP 5, other agents were behind me armed with shotguns. The subjects were dragged into the street and handcuffed.

The JBRTF obtained a search warrant that afternoon for the apartment, and seized a cache of weapons, approximately $800,000 in cash, and maps of previous banks they had robbed.

The pair were identified as brothers, former United States Marines. Each subject pled guilty and was sentenced to twenty years in federal prison.

POLICE

FBI Jackson Division
Jackson, Mississippi 1995

Assigned to the FBI Jackson Division, I supervised the FBI Jackson Division Fugitive Task Force (FTF) for a three year period.

The task force was composed of eight to twelve officers detailed from various law enforcement agencies: the Mississippi Highway Patrol, Mississippi Bureau of Narcotics (MBN), Jackson Police Department (JPD), Hinds County Sheriffs Office, and the Mississippi Department of Corrections (MDOC).

The FTF typical work schedule was 6 AM to 2 PM. On November 15, 1995, a very cold morning, I received information from our JPD task force officer that JPD Patrol Officer T.R. Jefferson failed to report to the precinct from the previous night shift. Officer Jefferson received his last call at approximately 9 PM.

At the conclusion of the shift at 10 PM, Officer Jefferson never reported to the precinct. JPD requested our assistance to locate Officer Jefferson. At approximately 8:30 AM, the FTF searched an obscure and abandoned drive-in movie theater parking lot and discovered the missing officer. Officer Jefferson was found laying on the trunk of his patrol car, shot three times in the back of the head. A brutal crime scene.

I immediately reported this information, established a crime scene, and awaited the arrival of the JPD Crime Lab and the Coroner.

This case remains unsolved.

STRIPPER

FBI Jackson, 1997

In June 1998, assigned to the FBI Jackson Division Violent Crime Squad. I received CI information that a Jackson drug gang contacted an associate, a hitman, Terry from Florida, to kill a rival drug dealer. CI advised Terry had done this type of work in the past and was paid well. NCIC inquiry indicated that Terry was wanted on firearms and narcotics charges. Terry was good at his work, considered armed and dangerous. I continued meeting with the CI and learned that when in Jackson, Terry frequented Starz, a strip club in south Jackson. On my way home on a Wednesday night, at approximately 6:30 PM., I stopped at Starz. Only a few customers at that hour. I identified myself to a dancer, "Passion", an attractive co-ed attending Jackson State University. I was offered free dinner, drinks, and a lap dance. I declined, but wanted/needed her cooperation. I showed her an arrest photograph of Terry and advised her that he was extremely dangerous. She agreed to call if he showed up. I told Passion I would pay her. The following Sunday morning at approximately 2:30 AM, my cell phone rang. My wife, Catherine, answered. I could hear loud rock music blaring through the receiver, a voice barely audible. The following memorable conversation ensued:

    Caller:
        "Is Agent Bisella there?"

    Catherine:
        "Who is this?

Caller:
"Passion".

Catherine:
"It's for you, it's Passion."

Passion told me that Terry entered Starz accompanied by an entourage. I was certain Terry and his crew were armed and typically were also wanted for charges as well. I contacted members of the Fugitive Task Force.

I was aware that Starz conducted a wand search for contraband upon entry, therefore, Terry and his group likely left their weapons in their cars. The FTF established surveillance in the Starz parking lot. A task force officer entered the club to positively ID Terry. At approximately 4 AM, Terry and his entourage exited Starz. As Terry approached his vehicle, he was apprehended without incident. Other members of his group were determined to have active warrants in Florida and Mississippi.

A few days later, I returned to Starz. Passion was compensated for her assistance.

JUSTICE

FBI Jackson, Fugitive Task Force, 1998

Solomon Oliver was a top narcotics dealer in Jackson, Mississippi, with connections and protection from a gang in Chicago.

The FTF was to serve several fugitive warrants for narcotics violations for Solomon Oliver. During the arrest, he fled in a vehicle and ran over a Mississippi Bureau of Narcotics (MBN) agent. The agent was hospitalized with severe injuries. Oliver's arrest was a priority.

FTF received CI information that Oliver would be in the vicinity of the Park Place Apartments in a gold Camaro. FTF established surveillance in the area. A vehicle matching the description entered the parking lot. A few seconds pass, the passenger door opens, Oliver exits and walks quickly to a ground floor apartment. A minute later, Oliver exited the apartment and jogged to the car. As he enters, the FTF approach and surround the vehicle. I was positioned at the passenger rear and task force officer Richard B. was positioned near the passenger door. (Richard, a former NFL defensive tackle, 6' 4", 280, was an incredible athlete). Oliver reached under the passenger seat, instinctively and seemingly in one motion, Richard kicked his right leg through the passenger window, glass shattering everywhere, pulled his leg out, reached in the car with his right hand, grabbed and lifted Oliver through the shattered window and slammed him onto the asphalt parking lot. Could not believe what I just witnessed. The driver was handcuffed, a semi-automatic pistol was retrieved from under Oliver's passenger seat. Oliver remained immobile on the ground, handcuffed, and taken to the hospital to have glass removed from his cheek.

Oliver's litany of charges would assure his stay in jail, or so I thought. In a week, his attorney petitioned the court, bail was lowered and Oliver was released. However, the streets are Darwinian. Several weeks later, Oliver was shot and killed in a drug deal.

This was the 1000 th arrest in a three year period for the FBI Jackson Fugitive Task Force.

INNOCENCE

FBI Jackson Division, 1998

Assigned to the FBI Jackson Division, Violent Crime Squad, I was requested by local law enforcement to assist in an investigation of a possible kidnapping. The victim was identified as Sarah Jones, a black female co-ed who attended a local community college. Sarah was a full-time student and held a part-time job. All witness accounts as well as interviews of family and friends indicated that she was a good person with no enemies. An interview of a fellow classmate and friend yielded information that Sarah sold nickel and dime bags of marijuana for side money. This was not by any means a lucrative enterprise, simply additional spending money. A classmate interview indicated that Sarah was to meet people from Florence, Alabama for a sale. I obtained emergency authorization for Sarah's cell phone records. Contemporaneously, I received a call that a body of a black female had been located in a wooded area in proximity to an office park in Rankin County, Mississippi. Upon arrival at the scene, the victim was positively identified as Sarah Jones. Sarah had duct tape wrapped tightly around her head covering both eyes, duct tape around her wrists and hog tied to her ankles. The index fingers and middle fingers of each hand were also duct taped together. The elaborate and unnecessary binding of the victim in this manner bore traits of a methodical torture or satanic ritual. Sarah was shot through both eyes, her body covered with ants and insects.

The investigation focused on her cell phone records which yielded several calls from a number in Florence, Alabama. Emergency authority to obtain subscriber information identified the subscriber as Lamar Collins and an associate, Leron Davis, each with lengthy and violent criminal histories. I traveled to Florence, Alabama to assist the Florence Police Department in the search for these individuals. Collins was arrested quickly without incident. Interrogation of Collins as well as crime scene forensic analysis, specifically, the vehicle of the deceased and hair recovered on the duct tape from the body of the deceased, corroborated that Davis was the shooter of Sarah Jones.

Davis was located in a crack house in Florence, Alabama. Florence Police Department SWAT made entry and quickly cleared the first floor and determined that Davis was in the attic. Davis was a black male, approximately 6'3", 250 pounds. Davis refused to surrender or comply with the SWAT commands. SWAT team entry to the attic was perilous given the small access point and serve as relatively easy targets for a desperate killer. Two SWAT officers crawled onto the attic floor in virtual darkness toward Davis's position, their weighted gear limiting their progress and signaling their location. Davis was concealed in the corner of the attic where the attic floor met the pitched metal roof. Davis was clearly enticing the officers to approach. I and other additional officers remained on the first floor and could only hear portions of verbal exchanges. As officers crawled within several feet of Davis in virtual darkness, Davis opened fire on the officers. The officers returned fire with H and K semi-automatic rifles. The firefight was close range, brief, and deadly. Davis was killed by SWAT.

The Assistant United States Attorney in Jackson, Mississippi requested that I obtain hair samples from Davis in order to establish a positive identification to those found in the victim's vehicle and on the duct tape. The following day, I contacted the funeral home where Davis was taken and prepared for viewing. The Funeral Director escorted me down the stairs to the basement of an antiquated, dimly lit, poorly equipped funeral home, with the ambiance of a haunted house. As we proceeded down the stairs to the basement, the Funeral Director stated, "he's draining in the basin".

I put on latex gloves and approached the deceased. The body was on a stainless steel embalming table positioned on an angle to drain. Davis had sustained 13 bullet wounds to his head, face, and upper torso. Having drawn hair samples in previous cases, there is a natural resistance from the follicle. However, extraction of hair samples from a dead body is particularly eerie in that the hair, upon extraction, easily slips out of the follicle which creates a macabre suction sound. The Funeral Director observed with amusement.

Sarah Jones was a genuinely good person, but had a chance encounter with evil. Sarah paid for this decision with her life.

GANG

FBI Jackson Division, 1998,

Assigned to the FBI Jackson Division, 1995 through 1999, I supervised the Organized Crime Drug Enforcement Task Force (OCDETF), the FBI Fugitive Task Force, and the National Center for Missing and Exploited Children Program.

An OCDETF investigation resulted in the arrest and conviction of eight drug gang members. Several entered guilty pleas, had been sentenced, and incarcerated at the Madison County Jail (MCJ), Madison Mississippi, a temporary detention center for federal inmates awaiting transfer to a Federal Correectional Institution (FCI). Pending their transfer, I traveled to MCJ to elicit cooperation from a gang leader, Anthony Hogan. After Hogan heard my offer, he grabbed his genitals and said, "Fuck you, I run this place", obviously unaware of his imminent transfer.

I asked the Warden of Hogan's status and was advised his transfer was imminent to FCI La Tuna, near El Paso, Texas, an institution noted for Mexican prison gangs, La Nuestra Familia, Mexican Mafia, and Texas Syndicate. Several months later I spoke to the Warden concerning another matter and was informed that, "Hogan was having difficulty assimilating."

Poetic justice.

COWARDS

FBI Jackson, circa 1998

I and other Fugitive Task Force (FTF) officers typically contacted sources and canvassed locations for next day assignments. One such routine day, I received radio information that there was a shooting on Bailey Avenue in Jackson, Mississippi. The FTF was in the vicinity and responded. Investigation and interviews at the scene indicated that two known drug gangs were involved in a mobile shooting from car to car. The two shooters were identified as Jarvis Brant and Nathaniel Cole. None of the perpetrators were wounded, however, two four year olds at a daycare center were wounded. The children were seriously injured and hospitalized but thankfully survived. News media coverage was statewide, every law enforcement agency was involved in the search for Brant and Cole.

The FTF actively contacted Confidential Informants (CI), anyone and everyone. Two days later, as we left a liquor store Brant was known to frequent, a task force officer received CI information concerning their current location. CI advised that Brant and Cole were in a room on the top floor of a hotel in downtown Jackson. The room was reserved in a fictitious name. I visited with the manager to review hotel guest information and determined Brant and Cole to be in Room 408. Brant and Cole had been in the room for two days and refused room/maid service. I reserved the room directly across the hall. We surveilled the room for a hour or so. Brant and Cole never left. CCTV indicated there were no visitors and the manager advised there were no incoming or outgoing calls for the duration of their stay. Since Brant and Cole had refused room service, I decided to enlist the assistance of the maid with the manager's concurrence. I requested that the maid knock on their door and ask if they wanted room service. A voice responded "no". As the maid turned to walk away, a voice yelled, "bring some extra towels".

I coordinated with the maid to knock on their door to deliver the towels, as the door was unlocked, she would step to the side and we would enter for the arrest. Brant or Cole would likely peer through the peephole so timing was critical. The maid knocked on the door, as the door lock was unlocked, we exited our room and hit the door. The impact of the entry caused Cole to be tossed across the room onto the floor in front of the television. Cole was immediately handcuffed. Brant was sitting on the bed, back to the headboard. Brant simultaneously reached for a 9mm pistol with his right arm and a baby with his left arm, which he held in front of himself. Several officers tackled and subdued Brant. The FTF JPD task force officer took custody of the child. The room was thick with a cloud of marijuana smoke. Drugs and paraphernalia were on the bed within arms reach of the baby. In minutes, the JPD task force officer determined the baby to be Brant's child with a girlfriend.

Brant and Cole were convicted in Hinds County Criminal Court and received substantial prison sentences. In the years since, each has since been released and rearrested multiple times. Brant and Cole have been in and out of state prison several times since this incident. Brant has escaped from prison at least once.

9/11

TDY-FBIHQ SIOC

In June 1999, I was transferred from the FBI Jackson Division to the FBI San Antonio Division, Austin Resident Agency. On Tuesday, September 11, 2001, I watched the World Trade Center attack in the FBI office. Having served in the FBI New York Office and witnessed the initial World Trade Center attack in 1993, I wanted to be there, to contribute, to be involved.

On Sunday, September 16, 2001, while attending church, I received a call from FBIHQ, Directors Office, asking whether I would be interested to join the investigative team of the 9/11 hijackers. I immediately agreed to report that night. I was one of ten FBI agents selected by the Director's Office to investigate the 9/11 hijackers.

Subsequent to 9/11, all domestic and international flights were grounded per Presidential and FAA authority. Domestic air service resumed intermittently on September 13/14, with limited service throughout the country. I reserved a flight from Austin, Texas to Washington D.C., Dulles Airport. The Austin airport was empty, heavily armed personnel patrolled throughout the terminal. I boarded the plane accompanied only by the pilot, co-pilot, and two flight attendants. The flight was non-stop to Dulles, I proceeded directly to the FBIHQ Strategic Information and Operations Center (SIOC). As I entered through the glass entrance door, I noticed a photograph of a former New York squad mate, Lenny Hatton, posted on the door. I worked with Lenny on the FBI New York Joint Bank Robbery Task Force. I was informed Lenny was among the missing and presumed dead.

SIOC functioned 24 hours a day, every federal agency in the country was represented. I was assigned to American Airlines Flight 77, which struck the Pentagon, specifically, two of the hijackers. On Monday, September 17, 2001, I traveled to the Pentagon. The site of destruction was overwhelming. The scent of airline fuel still remained in the air six days later. Our 9/11 investigative team received hourly updates from evidence recovery agents at each of the crash sites. The information contained therein was brutally graphic. We worked 18 to 20 hours a day for six weeks. Our collective work product was submitted directly to the FBI Director. All of us were dedicated to the effort and proud to be there.

Subsequent to this assignment, additional information and details were learned concerning FBI Special Agent Lenny Hatton. Lenny's actions on September 11 were incredibly heroic.

Leonard W. Hatton epitomized Fidelity, Bravery, Integrity. A former United States Marine, volunteer firefighter, honest, humble. All those who knew Lenny hold him in the highest esteem. I am honored and proud to have known Leonard W. Hatton.

FBI Special Agent Leonard W. Hatton is memorialized at the National 9/11 Memorial, on the site of the World Trade Center, South Pool, Panel S-26.

ABUSE

FBI, Austin Resident Agency
Austin, Texas

August 2005, a squad member asked for assistance executing a search warrant. The location to be searched was a two story residence owned by a single adult male, the Director of the local Boys and Girls Club. The interior and exterior was in pristine condition. Absolutely immaculate. A search of the residence yielded negative results. However, we located an upstairs room containing a single tantra chair and a VCR. The closet in this room was locked. The subject, seated on the living room sofa on the first floor, stared stoically straight ahead. He refused to provide the key or unlock the closet. He was told we will break the door to gain access. He relented and provided the key to the closet. A search of the closet found S and M devices, chains, whips, video cassettes, and most disturbing, a wooden soda bottle case containing bottles with apertures of varying sizes. The CA removed a random video and turned on the VCR. The video depicted the subject inserting the bottles in the rectums of two males laying across the tantra chair. I and the other agents were visibly upset and left the room. All items of evidentiary value were seized. The victims were immediately identified.

The subject remained free while the Assistant United States Attorney considered the appropriate charges. An arrest warrant was issued but the subject could not be located for approximately a week. A hotel manager near San Antonio contacted law enforcement and requested a welfare check at one of the rooms. Inside was a gruesome and macabre scene. The hotel room was saturated and splattered with blood. The subject had committed harakiri.

GRIEF

Pensacola, Florida
December 6, 2019

Post Bureau retirement, I wanted to continue as an investigator. On October 21, 2019, I began a term of employment as the Senior Investigator in the United States Attorney's Office, Pensacola, Florida. I rented a house bordering the North Hill section of Pensacola, approximately fifty yards from Baptist Hospital.

On the morning of Friday, December 6, 2019, at approximately 6:55 AM, I heard multiple sirens from all directions. Something tragic occurred. I walked outside and saw a fleet of ambulances, EMT vehicles, Pensacola Police Department vehicles, and Escambia County Sheriff's Office vehicles pulling in and around the emergency entrance to Baptist Hospital. I arrived at the United States Attorney's Office and learned that a terrorist active shooter attack occurred at the Pensacola Naval Air Station (NAS). There were three fatalities and at least eight wounded.

The United States Attorney for the Northern District of Florida, Lawrence A. Keefe, telephonically contacted me and advised that he was returning to Pensacola and needed a ride to the Naval Air Station. We arrived at the Naval Air Station and proceeded directly to the crime scene, a classroom facility, Building 633. Admittance was restricted, crime scene processing had not yet begun. FBI and NCIS agents were on scene.

United States Attorney Keefe was the primary federal law enforcement official responsible for any prosecution emanating from this terrorist attack. Mr. Keefe requested to view the crime scene. We were escorted to Building 633, as we approached, a United States Navy sailor, age 21, lay dead in the street from multiple gunshots. We walked to the entrance, NAS personnel required identification and a signature prior to entry. Upon entering, to our immediate right was the security/reception window. A United States Navy sailor, age 19, had been shot and killed sitting in his chair. We were informed the third victim, a United States Navy sailor, was in the rear seat of an Escambia County Sheriff's vehicle awaiting the arrival of EMT personnel and was transported to Baptist Hospital. The sailor, age 23, later died at Baptist Hospital. All were unarmed. We proceeded to the left, down the corridor, shattered glass and spent shell casings everywhere, the terrorist's bag with ammunition lay by a staircase. The terrorist, a Saudi national military aviation student, was deceased near the end of the corridor. He was shot and killed by responding Escambia County Sheriff's deputies.

We exited Building 633, Mr. Keefe received an investigative update from an agent. Mr. Keefe was advised the deceased Saudi terrorist attended pilot training with other Saudi military aviation students. The agent authoritatively advised that the Saudi nationals left the base immediately after the shooting but "were not involved in the attack." Mr. Keefe looked at me, I shook my head no. Mr. Keefe and I stepped to the side, I told him, 'he (the agent) is full of shit". First, he cannot and does not know whether the Saudi nationals were involved or not. To cavalierly state that the Saudi aviation students were not involved was not only premature, but the epitome of arrogance, incompetence, and negligence. Second, this was a terrorist attack on a United States military base, an active shooter incident, three unarmed United States Navy sailors were brutally murdered, eight others severely wounded. Interviews and accountability of all witnesses is mandatory and imperative, particularly, fellow Saudi nationals, classmates of the perpetrator. Charlatans and amateurs were in charge.

I recommended that all available law enforcement agencies be directed to locate these individuals. Mr. Keefe agreed and telephonically conferred with the United States Attorney General. Within hours, all Saudi nationals were located and returned to NAS.

Investigation determined that the Saudi nationals immediately fled the Pensacola Naval Air Station after the shooting, none informed NAS base personnel of the terrorist active shooter attack prior to leaving the crime scene. Disturbingly, on the evening prior to the attack, the shooter hosted a dinner at which he and three Saudi nationals watched videos of mass shootings in the United States.

On December 6, 2019, at approximately 6:30 PM, NAS and law enforcement personnel gathered outside Building 633 to mourn and salute the two deceased United States Navy sailors as their bodies were removed and escorted with full military honors.

Tragic. Shameful. Preventable.

www.ingramcontent.com/pod-product-compliance
Lightning Source LLC
Chambersburg PA
CBHW030507220526
45464CB00006B/2689